W9-AJP-823

K10

Storks
and Other Large Wading Birds

Book Author: Lisa Klobuchar
For World Book:
Editorial: Paul A. Kobasa, Maureen Liebenson, Christine Sullivan
Research: Andy Roberts, Loranne Shields
Graphics and Design: Melanie Bender, Sandra Dyrlund
Photos: Tom Evans, Sylvia Ohlrich
Permissions: Janet Peterson
Indexing: David Pofelski
Proofreading: Anne Dillon
Pre-press and Manufacturing: Carma Fazio, Anne Fritzinger, Steve Hueppchen, Madelyn Underwood

For information about other World Book publications, visit our Web site at
http://www.worldbook.com, or call 1-800-WORLDBK (967-5325).

For information about sales to schools and libraries, call 1-800-975-3250 (United States);
1-800-837-5365 (Canada).

World Book, Inc.
233 N. Michigan Avenue
Chicago, IL 60601
U.S.A.

Library of Congress Cataloging-in-Publication Data

Storks and other large wading birds
        p. cm. -- (World Book's animals of the world)
    Includes bibliographical references and index.
    ISBN 0-7166-1267-4 -- ISBN 0-7166-1261-5
    1. Ciconiiformes--Juvenile literature. 2. Storks--Juvenile
    literature. I. World Book, Inc. II. Series.
QL696 .C5S76 2005
598.3'4--dc22

                              2004019044

Printed in Malaysia
1 2 3 4 5 6 7 8 09 08 07 06 05

Picture Acknowledgments: Cover: © Kenneth W. Fink, Corbis; © Clem Haagner, Bruce Coleman Inc.; © Thomas Lazar, Animals Animals; © John Shaw, Bruce Coleman Inc.; © Roger Tidman, Corbis

© Erwin & Peggy Bauer, Bruce Coleman Inc. 15; © Wayne Bennett, Corbis 33; © Hal Beral, Corbis 4, 13; The Bridgeman Art Library 59; © Robin Chittenden, Corbis 5, 51; © Larry Ditto, Bruce Coleman Inc. 29; © Kenneth W. Fink, Bruce Coleman Inc. 61; © George Forrest, Bruce Coleman Inc. 39; © John Giustina, Bruce Coleman Inc. 9; © Phyllis Greenberg, Animals Animals 23; © Clem Haagner, Bruce Coleman Inc. 55; © Eric and David Hosking, Corbis 37; © Ernest Janes, Bruce Coleman Inc. 5, 41; © Peter Johnson, Corbis 7; © Gerard Lacz, Animals Animals 2, 17, 21; © Thomas Lazar, Animals Animals 43; © Robert Maier, Bruce Coleman Collection 25; © Joe McDonald, Bruce Coleman Inc. 9, 45; © Joe McDonald, Corbis 27; © McDonald Wildlife Photography/Animals Animals 19, 47, 57; © Fritz Polking, Bruce Coleman Inc. 31; © John Shaw, Bruce Coleman Inc. 9, 49; © Roger Tidman, Corbis 35; © Martin B. Withers, Frank Lane Picture Library/Corbis 9; © Klaus-Peter Wolf, Animals Animals 53.

Illustrations: WORLD BOOK illustration by John Fleck 11.

World Book's Animals of the World

Storks
and Other Large Wading Birds

Thermals help me fly!

World Book, Inc.
a Scott Fetzer company
Chicago

Contents

Back up half a mile.
Can you hear me
now?

Point your toes, stretch out your neck, don't forget to flap...

Can't a bird fish without being mistaken for a toupee?

What Are Storks and Other Large Wading Birds?

Storks and other large wading birds are birds that have long legs, necks, and bills. Scientists call these birds ciconiiforms *(suh KAHN ee uh fawrmz),* because they belong to the order Ciconiiformes. Most ciconiiforms wade through water searching for frogs, shellfish, insects, and other animals to catch and eat. A few of these birds, however, live in grasslands and do most of their hunting on dry land for small mammals, birds, and insects.

There are 19 species, or kinds, of stork. Storks have strong wings and stand from about 1½ to 5 feet (0.75 to 1.5 meters) high. Most of them live in wetlands—areas of land where the water level remains near or above the surface of the ground for most of the year.

Other ciconiiforms include egrets *(EE grehts),* herons *(HEHR uhnz),* bitterns *(BIHT uhrnz),* ibises *(EYE bihs sez),* and spoonbills. Flamingos are also classified as ciconiiforms by some scientists.

Yellow-billed storks

7

Where in the World Do Storks and Other Large Wading Birds Live?

These birds live in nearly all regions of the world, except in the polar areas. Most of these birds, however, tend to live in temperate or tropical places that are always warm.

Most stork species live in Europe, Asia, and Africa, but three species live in North, Central, or South America. These American species are the wood stork, the jabiru *(JAB uh roo),* and the maguari *(muh GWAH ree)* stork. The wood stork lives in the southeastern United States and parts of Central and South America. The jabiru and the maguari stork live in Central and South America.

A few species of stork raise their young in areas where the winters are cold, but these storks migrate to warmer regions in winter. For example, white storks spend the summer months in northern Europe and western Asia. They then fly to Africa, India, or southern China for the winter.

8

Jabiru

Wood stork

Marabou

Cattle egret

What Is Special About the Bill of These Birds?

The bills of ciconiiforms are adapted to the special ways in which these birds eat.

White storks have a really long, pointed bill. The white stork can quickly open and shut the upper and lower parts of its bill. The bird uses its bill like tweezers, to snatch up small, fast-moving rodents and insects and slippery fish.

Wood storks and spoonbills both find food in shallow, muddy water, where it is difficult to see prey. These birds have bills that are very sensitive to touch. When they feel prey, their bill snaps closed so fast that the prey has no chance of escaping.

Herons locate their prey by sight before they spear it using their sharp bill. Shoebills use their large bill to catch large prey.

A flamingo uses its long neck to lower its head into shallow water. When its head is upside down, the flamingo "shakes" it from side to side, collecting food from the water in its curved bill.

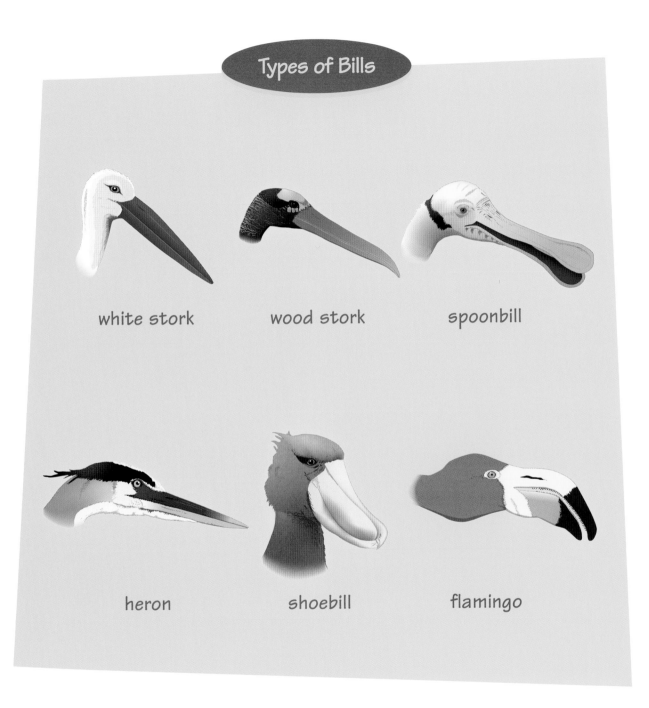

Types of Bills

white stork

wood stork

spoonbill

heron

shoebill

flamingo

11

Do Storks Have Voices?

Most storks are fairly silent birds. In general, birds make calls and songs with a sound-making organ at the bottom of their windpipe. This organ is called the syrinx *(SIHR ihngks)*. The syrinx of storks is not as well developed as that of some other kinds of birds, however, and most species of stork are able to make only soft grunting, hissing, and whistling noises.

Even without a loud voice, storks can still make noise. They do this by clattering their bills. During breeding season, a male or female stork may make clattering noises with its bill to attract a mate.

Both the male and female of some species of stork have a pouch of skin that hangs from their neck. Storks use their throat pouch in mating displays (actions taken to attract attention). First, a stork throws its head backwards. This position makes the throat pouch tighten. This tightening causes the throat pouch to act as an amplifier—that is, it makes sound louder. Then the bird claps the upper and lower parts of its bill together to produce a loud rattling sound. People have described the sound as being similar to the noise made by a machine gun. And it is loud! Clattering can be heard from about ½ mile (1 kilometer) away.

Jabiru

Which Storks Are on the Cleanup Crew?

Three kinds of stork are very helpful when it comes to keeping their surroundings clean. These are the marabou *(MAR uh boo)* of Africa and the greater adjutant *(AJ uh tuhnt)* and lesser adjutant of India and Southeast Asia. These storks eat carrion, the flesh of dead animals.

Marabous and adjutants find the carcasses (bodies of dead animals) by soaring around in the sky and searching the ground below. When they locate a carcass, they glide down toward it. Usually other carrion-eating birds, such as vultures, are also feeding on the carcass.

Marabou storks
with carrion

Are Storks Good at Flying?

The answer is both yes and no. Because storks are large and heavy birds, getting up into the sky and staying there is hard work for them. If storks had to flap their wings a lot while flying, as smaller birds do, they would have a pretty hard time. But storks have found a way to fly high and far without having to work so hard. When storks fly, they often glide on warm columns of air called thermals.

Thermals form when air comes in contact with land that has become warm by absorbing a lot of heat from the sun. The air is warmed by the land and rises as a thermal.

Storks have to flap their wings to take off. But, once they are in the air, they can spread their large wings and let the thermals carry them higher and higher. Storks may ride thermals beyond a height of 3,500 feet (1,070 meters). While gliding on thermals, storks do not have to flap their wings much, which means they save a lot of energy.

White stork

Where Do Storks Spend the Winter?

Most species of stork live in tropical areas, where the weather is warm all the time. These storks stay in the same area year round. But white storks and black storks are different—they are long-distance travelers.

The breeding ranges of both the black stork and the white stork include areas in Europe and Asia that have cold winters. As winter approaches in these regions, the storks begin a long journey called a migration *(my GRAY shuhn)* to places where the weather is warm. Some storks migrate to the southern tip of Africa. Others fly eastward to India or south to southern China.

Storks choose a route that has good thermals. Because thermals usually do not form over water, migrating storks fly mostly over land. When traveling from Europe to Africa, storks cross the Mediterranean Sea at points where the sea is narrow, or the birds travel over the land that surrounds the sea. The two main migration routes followed by storks are near the Strait of Gibraltar between Spain and Africa and across the Middle East.

European white storks
in a tree in Kenya

19

What Is Special About a Stork's Nest?

When it comes to nests, storks seem to believe that bigger is better. Storks' nests are large platforms made of sticks and lined with grass, rags, paper, and other materials. Storks build their nests in trees or on cliff ledges. Some types of stork will build a nest on the ground. White storks build nests on rooftops, church steeples, towers, chimneys, and telephone poles. Many people like having storks nearby, so they provide the storks with nice places to build nests, such as platforms on rooftops or special nest towers.

Often a pair of storks will come back to the same nest year after year. Each year, they add more material to it. Both the male and female stork help to build the nest. Some nests are very old and very big—as large as 9 feet (2.7 meters) deep and 6 feet (2 meters) across.

Rooftop nests
of white storks

How Do Storks Say "I Love You"?

Many storks share a special dance with their mates at the beginning of the breeding season. When white storks migrate south for the winter, they separate from their mates. But, when they return to their breeding ground, they usually go back to their old nest. There, they often meet their mate from the year before.

Most storks begin a dance by bobbing their head. Then the male and female stand bill to bill, taking turns bobbing and nodding their head at each other. Often, storks make loud rattling noises during this display by snapping their bill.

No one knows what this dance really means. It may be a way for a pair to get to know each other again after a long separation. It may be a stork's way of showing how fit it is—a way of indicating, "I'll be a good parent." But it also seems to be an important way for the two storks to show they are now a team.

Wood stork
courtship display

How Long Does It Take for a Baby Stork to Grow Up?

A female stork usually lays three to seven white eggs. An egg laid by a white stork is a little larger than a chicken's egg. The stork chicks hatch in about four to six weeks. Newly hatched storks are helpless and covered with fluffy feathers. The chicks need a lot of food. The parents find and eat the food. Then they come back to the nest and spit up the food for the chicks to eat.

Most young storks get their first set of feathers when they are 8 or 9 weeks old. Then they are ready to leave the nest. Some may still hang around the nest for some time, begging for food. But, the young of storks that migrate must be able to take care of themselves by the time they leave on the southward journey in the fall.

Storks are ready to mate and have their own babies by the time they are about 4 years old.

White storks

Which Are the Largest Ciconiiforms?

The largest ciconiiforms are storks. And, of the storks, the largest species is the African marabou. These birds can reach a height of 5 feet (1.5 meters). In general, for all ciconiiforms, the female of a species is slightly smaller than the male, but the difference is not great.

Of the other members of the ciconiiforms, one large species is the goliath heron. This bird also comes from Africa, and it towers over all other herons. It stands more than 4½ feet (1.4 meters) high.

Goliath herons eat mostly fish. Their size allows them to wade out to deeper water than can many other wading birds, so they can catch bigger fish that swim farther from the shore. When a goliath heron spots a fish, the bird thrusts its head and neck down into the water with lightning speed. The goliath either snatches up the fish by clamping it in its bill, or the heron spears the fish with its pointy bill. It kills the fish before swallowing it by laying the fish on a mat of floating plants and stabbing it.

26

Goliath heron

Which Are the Smallest Ciconiiforms?

The smallest storks, such as the hammerkop stork and the African openbill, grow to a height of around 24 inches (60 centimeters).

But, of all the ciconiiforms, the least bittern of North and South America is the smallest. It is 11 to 14 inches (28 to 36 centimeters) tall. The least bittern hunts for fish and small animals among the cover of cattails and reeds.

The least bittern, like all bitterns, is a shy bird. When frightened, bitterns freeze and point their bills straight up into the air. The bittern has a dark brown stripe on its chest that helps it to blend in perfectly with surrounding grasses when it is in this pose.

This bird can stay completely still for some time. If its enemy changes position, the bittern may move very slowly so that its striped chest is always facing the enemy.

Least bittern

What Is a Colony?

Black storks, woolly-necked storks, and jabirus generally live alone, and so do bitterns and a few species of ibis. Only during the breeding season do these birds nest in pairs.

But, most storks and herons nest and feed in large groups, called colonies. Sometimes the colony is made up of only one species of bird. Often, however, storks and herons nest in large groups made up of several species. For example, storks, ibises, spoonbills, herons, and egrets may all form one nesting colony. Such colonies can be made up of thousands of birds.

These birds usually build their nests in trees. In some colonies, the smaller birds build their nests lower down in the trees, and the larger birds get the higher branches. After the chicks have hatched, the colony becomes a noisy, smelly place. Some species, especially the egrets, are not very nice neighbors. They often steal the food—and even the nests—of other birds in the colony.

Colony of egrets
and herons

What Is Life Like in an Egret's Nest?

It is not always "home, sweet home" in an egret's nest. In fact, family life for egrets can get pretty nasty.

The female egret will most often lay three eggs that are each about the size of a chicken's egg (or a little larger). These eggs are whitish or pale blue in color and are laid one at a time a few days apart. This means that each of the chicks is a slightly different age. This is fine for the first chicks to hatch, but the last chick to hatch can be in for a tough time.

The oldest two chicks have a head start, so they are bigger and stronger than the youngest. The three chicks compete for food from the parents, and the youngest of the chicks often goes hungry. It may fall further behind in growth and become weaker because it does not get enough to eat. Often, the older chicks pick on the youngest and, before long, they may even kill it.

This strategy, however, does mean that at least one or two egret chicks usually survive, even when food is scarce.

Snowy egret feeding chicks

Why Do Herons and Egrets Change "Clothes"?

Many members of the heron family, which includes egrets, grow new feathers during the breeding season. Other members have legs and bills that change color. And, still others have feathers, legs, and bills that all change! These changes start happening before the mating season. Birds of both sexes grow showy feathers called breeding plumage and change colors to attract mates.

A small heron called the squacco heron sprouts long, fluffy black-and-white feathers all around its head and neck as breeding plumage. The agami heron of South America grows light blue, ribbonlike feathers on its head and gray-blue plumes on its back. Great egrets grow large, beautiful, lacy feathers from their heads, necks, and backs. The cattle egret's white body feathers get pale tan highlights, and its legs and bill turn from yellow to a bright orange color.

But the new "clothes" do not last for long. After the young are raised, the parents' showy plumes drop off and are replaced by regular plumage. Their legs and bills turn back to their original color, as well.

Squacco heron showing
breeding plumage

Why Is That Flamingo So Colorful?

The flamingo is a beautiful bird with stiltlike legs and a long, curved neck. In the wild, flamingos vary in color from bright red to pale pink.

To feed, a flamingo puts its head upside down beneath shallow water. Then it moves its head from side to side to catch and filter out food from the water with its bill.

One food flamingos like to eat is algae *(AL jee)*. Some of the types of algae that flamingos feed on contain pigments called carotenoids *(kuh ROT uh noydz)*. These carotenoids make the flamingo's feathers their pink or red color.

When flamingos are kept in a zoo, the birds are often fed a special diet that contains these carotenoids. Without the special diet, the flamingo's feathers would fade to off-white. Feathers molted (shed) by a flamingo soon fade to off-white, as well.

Flamingo feeding

What Are Some Fishing Tricks Used by Ciconiiforms?

Anyone who has ever been fishing knows that there are a lot of ways to trick fish into biting. Egrets, herons, and spoonbills have a few tricks of their own. And they work!

Some egrets wriggle their feet and stir up the mud on the bottom of a pond. These actions attract the prey or startle it into movement.

The green heron also uses bait to attract fish. It drops insects, worms, twigs, or feathers onto the surface of the water. When a fish approaches the bait, the heron grabs the fish.

Spoonbills have a long bill that is flattened at the end. The birds sweep their bills from side to side in the water to produce tiny water currents. Small prey gets trapped in the currents just long enough for the spoonbill to snatch it.

Green heron fishing

Who Hunts Under a "Tent"?

The black heron of Africa has an unusual way of hunting. It crouches in the water and raises its wings over its head to make a kind of tent. From under its raised wings, it peers down into the water and grabs and eats its prey.

No one knows exactly how this behavior helps the black heron catch fish. Perhaps the fish swim toward the shade created by the heron's wings because it looks like a safe place to hide. Or, maybe the "tent" pose makes it harder for fish to recognize the heron as an enemy. Another possibility is that the raised wings lessen the glare from the sun off the water's surface, which helps the heron see its prey more clearly under the water.

Black heron fishing

41

Which Bird Comes Knocking for Its Dinner?

What would you think about a bird that knocks at its prey's door to get the prey to come out? Would you say that the bird is very polite or very sneaky?

The white ibis especially likes crayfish, a type of freshwater animal that looks like a lobster. During the summer, crayfish escape the heat by burrowing under moist soils along the shoreline. This makes it harder for the ibis to find the crayfish. But the ibis has figured out a solution. A hungry white ibis creeps up to a crayfish burrow. The burrow has a mound of mud around the entrance, made when the crayfish dug out its burrow.

The ibis picks up bits of dried mud from the mound and drops them, one at a time, down the hole. Then it quietly waits. Soon, the crayfish starts to dig itself out from the mud the ibis has dropped into its prey's burrow. When the crayfish peeks out of the burrow opening, the ibis grabs it. The bird beats the crayfish on the ground to break off its legs and claws and then swallows the rest whole.

White ibis

Who Chases Fish?

It is difficult to catch a fish as it darts through the water. That is why, to avoid scaring their prey, most herons and egrets stand very still in the water when they hunt fish, moving only their eyes. However, as is usual in nature, there are exceptions to this rule. Some egrets actively chase fish when they hunt, rather than waiting for the fish to come to them.

One of the most active wading birds is the reddish egret. This egret will run and hop in the shallow water where it pursues swimming fish. It often holds out one or both of its wings as it chases its prey, probably to help the bird keep its balance.

Reddish egret fishing

Which Large Wading Birds Are Active at Night?

Most large wading birds are active during the day. But a few types hunt and feed at night. When other birds are settling in for a good night's sleep, these birds are just waking up. You might call these birds "night owls."

During the evening and night, the black-crowned night heron crouches along the edge of the water and lunges for fish, frogs, and water insects. It also eats the eggs and chicks of other water birds. Night herons have large eyes and good night vision.

The boat-billed heron is also active at night. It has even larger eyes than the night heron. It sometimes uses its huge bill to scoop up prey from the water.

Black-crowned
night heron

Who Has a Bill That Looks Like a Shoe?

The first thing you will notice if you ever see a shoebill is its huge, curved, hooked bill. People thought this bill resembled a wooden shoe like those worn by people in Holland, and that is how the bird got its name. This bill is the perfect tool for scooping up long, eel-like fish, called lungfish, which live in muddy ponds.

Shoebills live in central and eastern Africa in swampy habitats. Both males and females of this species stand about 4 feet (1.2 meters) tall and have gray feathers. The top of their head has a small tuft of feathers called a crest. These birds live alone and build their nest on small islands in wetlands, or on floating mats of plant material.

Shoebill

Which Birds Are Willing to Stick Out Their Necks to Fly?

When herons fly, they fly with their long legs extended behind them, but with their head tucked between their shoulders. Their long neck bends into an "S" shape, so their head is close to their body.

The shoebill also flies with its head close to its body. But, other ciconiiforms fly with their neck extended. Ibises fly this way. Storks also fly with their neck extended.

Because certain storks and herons can look alike, checking for the position of the head and neck when these birds are in flight is a good way to tell them apart.

Scarlet ibis

How Do These Birds Keep Cool?

Birds, like all animals, have to keep their bodies at a comfortable temperature in order to survive. They cannot get too hot or too cold. And, because most wading birds live in warm areas, staying cool can be hard for them. Many wading birds have, however, developed interesting ways to keep cool.

Of course, a wading bird can always just go wading. Anyone who has ever dipped his or her feet into a stream or pond knows that is a good way to cool off. In addition, many wading birds cool down by a type of "panting"—these birds flutter their throat pouches to get rid of body heat. They may also lift their wings slightly away from their bodies to let more heat escape.

Although very young wading birds are not as active as adults, they can overheat, as well. A nest can be a very hot place. Some wading birds have found ways to help their young stay cool. An adult shoebill, for instance, will carry water back to its nest in its large bill and sprinkle the water over its young or its eggs.

Marabou stork with
throat pouch

Who Builds Their Own Birdhouse?

The hammerkop, or hammerhead, is a drab brown bird that looks a lot like a heron. The hammerkop's nest is a huge, dome-shaped house made of sticks. The inside of the house is lined with mud. These complex nests may be as large as 5 feet (1.5 meters) across. A small hole serves as an entrance to this nest, and inside there is a large nesting chamber.

Over time, hammerkops continue to add more sticks and mud to their nest. The hammerkop nest is so large, smaller birds, such as sparrows, sometimes build their own nests in spaces they find between the sticks.

The hammerkop gets its name because of the short crest of feathers that sticks straight out from the back of its head. Both male and female hammerkops have this crest. Along with its pointed bill, the crest makes the bird's head look like the head of a hammer.

Hammerkops
with nest

Who Hangs Around with Cattle?

If you see a small, white bird sitting comfortably on the back of a cow, an ox, or a buffalo, it is likely you are looking at a cattle egret. Cattle egrets sometimes hunt like other wading birds, catching fish and frogs along the water's edge. But, most often, they follow herds of livestock to eat the grasshoppers that are stirred up by the cattle's hoofs. They also eat flies and other biting creatures that are pests to the cows. Cattle egrets also can be found searching for things to eat at garbage dumps.

Cattle egrets originally lived only in Africa. But, during the mid-1900's, they slowly began to increase their flying range to North and South America as well. In fact, cattle egrets can be found now almost anywhere there is farming or animal herding. Today, they are one of the most widespread and common wading birds.

African buffalo with cattle egret

Which Bird Can Be Found in Ancient Tombs?

The ancient Egyptians worshiped many gods and goddesses. One of their most beloved gods was named Thoth *(thohth* or *toht).* Thoth was the patron of writing, astronomy, mathematics, law, magic, and healing. He was often drawn having the body of a man and the head of an ibis.

Ancient Egyptians mummified, or preserved, dead ibises and gave them as offerings to the gods. To mummify an ibis, the body of the dead bird was wrapped in many layers of cloth bandages. Some ibis mummies were placed in ibis-shaped coffins. Archaeologists have found large numbers of mummified ibises in ancient Egyptian sites.

The species of ibis most commonly mummified by the ancient Egyptians was the sacred ibis. The sacred ibis has white feathers and a bare black skin on its head and neck. This bird was common in Egypt during ancient times. It still lives today in many areas of Africa.

Thoth depicted with an ibis head

Are These Birds in Danger?

Altogether, about a dozen large wading birds are considered endangered. This means that they could become extinct. The rarest of these birds are the crested ibis, the giant ibis, and the dwarf olive ibis.

In the past, some of these birds, especially the egrets, were nearly wiped out because people killed them for their beautiful plumes. But laws were then passed to protect the birds, and some species have recovered. In some parts of the world, though, storks and their relatives are still hunted for their meat and feathers. The milky stork, for example, is a vulnerable species that is still being hunted in Asia.

Pesticides, or poisons used to kill insects, also harm these birds and their eggs. The birds also sometimes crash into electric power lines and are electrocuted.

However, the biggest threat these birds face today is the loss of wetlands. When people drain wetlands to make land for farms or houses, these birds lose their homes and their food source.

Milky stork

Large Wading Bird
Fun Facts

→ The jabiru, a stork of South America, has a huge bill. Its bill can be as long as 12 inches (30 centimeters).

→ The wood stork can snap its bill shut within 25 milliseconds of sensing a fish. That is the fastest known reflex action for any vertebrate (animal with a backbone).

→ It takes nearly four months after hatching for a young shoebill to begin flying.

→ The long toes of wading birds help support them when walking on mud.

→ The stork is considered to bring good luck in many parts of the world. In many areas of Europe, rituals and celebrations to welcome the storks back after wintering in Africa are observed each year in the spring.

Glossary

algae Simple plantlike organisms that usually live in water.

breed To produce offspring.

burrow A hole dug in the ground by an animal for shelter.

carrion The flesh of dead animals.

ciconiiforms The order to which storks and other large wading birds belong.

colony A large group of animals that live together.

crest A tuft or comb of feathers on the head of a bird.

endangered In danger of extinction, or dying out.

habitat An area where an animal lives, such as a grassland or wetland.

migrate To travel from one region to another with a change in the season.

molt To shed feathers, skin, hair or other old growths before a new growth happens.

mummify To preserve a body by treating it with special chemicals and wrapping it in cloth strips.

pesticides Chemicals that are used to kill harmful insects.

pigment The substance that colors the tissues of an animal or plant.

plumage The feathers of a bird.

syrinx The sound-making organ at the bottom of the windpipe in birds.

thermal A mass of warm air that forms over land during the daytime and rises high into the sky.

tropical Refers to the tropics, areas that are warm throughout the year.

wetland An area, such as a marsh or swamp, that has water on the surface for all or much of the year.

Index

(**Boldface** indicates a photo or illustration.)

For more information about Storks and Other Large Wading Birds, try these resources:

Herons, by Frank Staub, Lerner Publications, 1997.
Storks: Majestic Migrators, by Eulalia Garcia, Gareth Stevens Publishing, 1996.
Wading Birds: From Herons to Hammerheads, by Sara Swan Miller, Sagebrush Bound, 2003.

http://animaldiversity.ummz.umich.edu/site/accounts/classification/Ciconiiformes.html

http://www.earthlife.net/birds/ciconiiformes.html

Large Wading Bird Classification

Scientists classify animals by placing them into groups. The animal kingdom is a group that contains all the world's animals. Phylum, class, order, and family are smaller groups. Each phylum contains many classes. A class contains orders, an order contains families, and a family contains individual species. Each species also has its own scientific name. (The abbreviation "spp." after a genus name indicates that a group of species from a genus is being discussed.) Here is how the animals in this book fit into this system.

Animals with backbones and their relatives (Phylum Chordata)
Birds (Class Aves)
Storks and other wading birds (Order Ciconiiformes)
Flamingo* (Family Phoenicopteridae)

Flamingo . . . .*Phoeniconaias* spp.

Hammerkop (or hammerhead; Family Scopidae)

Hammerkop (or hammerhead) . . . .*Scopus umbretta*

Herons and their relatives (Family Ardeidae)

Agami heron . . . .*Agamia agami*
Black-crowned night heron . . . .*Nycticorax nycticorax*
Boat-billed heron . . . .*Cochlearius cochlearius*
Cattle egret . . . .*Bubulcus ibis*
Goliath heron . . . .*Ardea goliath*
Great egret . . . .*Casmerodius albus*
Green heron . . . .*Butorides virescens*
Least bittern . . . .*Ixobrychus exilis*
Plumed egrets . . . .*Egretta* spp
   Black heron . . . .*Egretta ardesiaca*
   Reddish egret . . . .*Egretta rufescens*
   Snowy egret . . . .*Egretta thula*
Squacco heron . . . .*Ardeola ralloides*

Ibises and spoonbills (Family Threskiornithidae)

Crested ibis . . . .*Nipponia nippon*
Dwarf olive ibis . . . .*Bostrychia bocagei*
Giant ibis . . . .*Thaumatibis gigantea*
Roseate spoonbill . . . .*Ajaia ajaja*
Sacred ibis . . . .*Threskiornis aethiopicus*
White ibises . . . .*Eudocimus* spp.
   Scarlet ibis . . . .*Eudocimus ruber*
   White ibis . . . .*Eudocimus albus*

Shoebill (Family Balaenicipitidae)

Shoebill . . . .*Balaeniceps rex*

Storks (Family Ciconiidae)

Ciconias . . . .*Ciconia* spp.
   Black stork . . . .*Ciconia nigra*
   Maguari . . . .*Ciconia maguari*
   Woolly-necked stork . . . .*Ciconia episcopus*
   White stork . . . .*Ciconia ciconia*
Leptoptilos . . . .*Leptoptilos* spp.
   Greater adjutant . . . .*Leptoptilos dubius*
   Lesser adjutant . . . .*Leptoptilos javanicus*
   Marabou . . . .*Leptoptilos crumeniferus*
Jabiru . . . .*Jabiru mycteria*
Wood storks . . . .*Mycteria* spp.
   Milky stork . . . .*Mycteria cinerea*
   Wood stork . . . .*Mycteria americana*
   Yellow-billed stork . . . .*Mycteria ibis*

* Some scientists place flamingos into their own order, Phoenicopteriformes.